Another Name For Earth

O Outro Nome da Terra

O OUTRO NOME DA TERRA

Eugénio de Andrade

ANOTHER NAME FOR EARTH

Translated by
Alexis Levitin

QED Press
Fort Bragg, California

Another Name for Earth / O Outro Nome da Terra
By Eugénio de Andrade, translated by Alexis Levitin

QED Press
155 Cypress Street
Fort Bragg, CA 95437
(707) 964-9520 Fax: (707) 964-7531

Publisher's Cataloging-in-Publication

Andrade, Eugénio de.
[O Outro Nome da Terra. English and Portuguese]
Another Name for Earth = O Outro Nome da Terra / Eugénio de Andrade : translated by Alexis Levitin
p. cm.
ISBN 0-936609-37-0
LCCN 95-72726
1. Andrade, Eugénio de.— Translations into English.
I. Levitin, Alexis, tr. II. Title: O Outro Nome da Terra.
III. Title: Another Name for Earth.
PQ9261.A64 1996 869.1'42
I95-20847

Cover design and illustration by Mark Gatter

Publication of this book was supported by a Translation Grant from The National Library and Book Institute of Lisbon, Portugal *(Instituto da Biblioteca Nacional e do Livro, Lisboa)*, and with the assistance of the Camões Institute of Lisbon *(Instituto Camões)*.

MINISTÉRIO DA EDUCAÇÃO
INSTITUTO CAMÕES

Printed in Canada

First edition

Acknowledgments

I would like to thank Eugénio de Andrade for his patient collaboration over the years. I would also like to thank Clara Pires, the translator's ideal consultant, for her insight, wisdom, and good humor. Finally, I am happy to acknowledge the support of the State University of New York at Plattsburgh and the Gulbenkian Foundation of Lisbon, Portugal, with special thanks to Dr. José Blanco.

Some of these translations have appeared in the following magazines and journals:

Beacons
Crab Creek Review
Graham House Review
Home Planet News
the new renaissance
Osiris
Seneca Review
Translation
Webster Review
Confrontation
Delos
Hawaii Review
Metamorphoses
Nimrod
Poetry Miscellany
Tinta y Sombra
Visions International
Wordsmith

Three of these translations have appeared in the anthology, *Literary Olympians 1992*, edited by Elizabeth Bartlett, Ford-Brown & Co., Boston, 1992

Ao Miguel, ao Gil, ao Dario
— que tornam a terra mais habitável

For Miguel, for Gil, for Dario
— who make the earth more livable

Introduction

Eugénio de Andrade is probably Portugal's best known contemporary poet. His work has been translated into over twenty languages, including Spanish, French, Italian, Greek, Serbo-Croatian, Rumanian, Bulgarian, Hungarian, Czech, Russian, German, Dutch, Swedish, Norwegian, and, of course, English. A dozen volumes of his work have appeared in France and fifteen volumes have been published in Spain, where he has been translated not only into Spanish, but also into Bable (an Asturian dialect), Catalan, and Galego. In the United States, my translations of his work have appeared in close to 150 literary magazines, a handful of anthologies, and in five books prior to this one: *Inhabited Heart* (Perivale Press, 1985), *White on White* (QRL, 1987), *Memory of Another River* (New Rivers Press, 1988), *Slopes of a Gaze* (Apalachee Press, 1992), which won the first Fernando Pessoa Translation Prize from Columbia University's Translation Center, and *Solar Matter* (QED Press, 1995).

Eugénio de Andrade has received numerous literary awards, including the "Prémio da Critica" from the International Association of Literary Critics in 1986, the "Prémio D. Dinis" in 1988, the "Grande Prémio de Poesia" of the Portuguese Writers' Association in 1989, and the

French "Priz Jean Malrieu" in 1989. Marguerite Yourcenar refers to "the well-tempered clavier" of his poems; the Mexican poet Angel Flores calls his "a classic language, that is to say, an enduring language that becomes richer at every reading"; and the Spanish poet and critic Angel Crespo writes that "his voice was born to baptize the world." More than a dozen books dealing with his work have appeared in Portugal, and he has garnered considerable critical attention in Spain, Italy, France, and Brazil. In November, 1993, an international conference to honor the poet was held in Porto, the city in northern Portugal where he has lived for more than forty years. In conjunction with the conference, The Fundação Eugénio de Andrade published a selection of thirty of his poems in Portuguese, accompanied by translations into French, Spanish, and English. It was a fitting commemoration of de Andrade's seventieth birthday and fiftieth year as a published poet.

O Outro Nome da Terra (Another Name for Earth) was launched in November, 1988, just after the poet's return from a forty-day reading tour of the United States and Canada. It had been his first visit to the USA and the first such extended tour by a Portuguese writer. Within a year, *O Outro Nome da Terra* appeared in a Spanish version in Valencia, and a year later the French translation was published in Paris. Over the last six years, nearly all the poems in this collection have appeared in various literary magazines in the USA.

Eugénio de Andrade is always a poet of the four elements, with a great predilection for matter and an aversion to abstraction. A clue to the special angle of this book, however, can best be found in the dedication: "For Miguel, for Gil, for Dario — who make the earth more livable." Dario, a new friend at the time, is a photographer whose attentive eye helped the poet focus again on the textures of matter, "the rough or sweet skin of things." Together they went on to publish a book in which the coarse touch of rock, the brightness of white-washed walls, and the richness of fields of flowers or of grain were celebrated in photographs and poetic prose. Gil had been a youngster playing in the streets of Eugénio's neighborhood some thirty years earlier when the poet befriended him. Clearly he is a reminder of the past, always associated with the lost youth of the poet himself, but he is also the progenitor of the future. For Miguel, his son, is the poet's beloved godchild and protégé: it is Miguel who most powerfully carries the poet back to the simple and joyful sensory world of childhood, that lost paradise which he continues to seek and recreate in his verse.

In this collection, the figure of Miguel is discernible in at least six poems. The book opens with a rhetorical question addressed to this child, this figure of renewal and hope: "Toward what star are you growing, / my son, toward what early morning star?" And the poem ends with the hope that there is still time "for me and that cloud, that high cloud / to go with you." It is apparent, then, from the outset, that the poet hopes this child can somehow carry him forward, towards that "early morning star." In the next poem, "In a Photograph," the poet's desire to arrest the passing of time is made explicit when he pleads:

Just stay, just stay like this:
make of your gaze
time without time.

And in the following poem, contemplating the inevitable transformation of infant into child, child into adolescent, he ruefully remarks that "your tiny feet no longer linger / on my chest…for you are growing." He then concludes with the mysteriously resonant image of the book's title: "Now you are the other name for earth / or simply for eternity." A bit later, in a poem called "City," the speaker walks along, "the child's hand in mine…exorcising shadows, summoning forth…a sun still fresh." And as they go forward, "his hand gives light to mine." The next poem reflects on the general phenomenon of children growing up, and here the poet resists the shadow of loss by absorbing the children into himself: "They are growing in my thread-bare heart." And once again he counters the logic of time with his insistence: "only children do not die." Finally, in the poem "With You," as so often, the poet finds consolation and the promise of eternity in his art itself:

No love is sterile, a son
can be a star, a line of poetry.

In these poems we see the poet's joy at beholding the wonder of pure physical existence before him, in the innocent or even pre-innocent form of an infant, a small child, as free of abstraction as an animal. We also see his nostalgia provoked by this vision and his desire to somehow burst free of time and its limitations into a vision of eternity — not the abstract concept, but rather the living, reborn flesh of this eternal earth.

Certainly a sense of human finiteness and loss lurks throughout these poems. The sea, that immensity to which we must return, to which we must surrender our individual self, appears often in this collection. And there is an array of other images suggesting loss: hands as the "porous home of summer," a premonition that "perhaps this is the last summer, so slack the weave of my desire," language seen as "the snuffed-out heart of the fire," autumn "where the last light of the cicadas sings," the plaint of "tonight the rain got to my very bones," a glimpse of his own "dismantled heart," a poem called "Epitaph," another depicting a vision "like death in childhood / just as tall, as white, as hoarse", and, at the end, the angry, fragmented poem, "Rose of the World": "Burnt…Filthy from so many words…Obscene rose." Yet this painful farewell concludes ambiguously, perhaps on a reluctantly positive note:

> Obscene rose. Shared.
> Loved.
> Wounded mouth, nobody's breath.
>
> Almost nothing.

Despite these darker intimations and reflections, the presiding spirit of this volume seems to be one of affirmation of the life of the senses, of the pleasure of human flesh, joyous under a warm sun and on this textured earth.

And this spirit is reconfirmed through a vision of childhood, today's child and yesterday's remembered self, together resonating with eternity.

Alexis Levitin
Plattsburgh, NY
New York, NY
.May 1995

Another Name For Earth

O Outro Nome da Terra

O Outro Nome da Terra

Cumplicidades do Verão

Another Name For Earth

Complicities of Summer

Rose of the World

COM ESSA NUVEM

Para que estrela estás crescendo,
filho, para que estrela matutina?
Diz-me, diz-me ao ouvido,
se é tempo ainda,
eu e essa nuvem, essa nuvem alta,
de irmos contigo.

WITH THAT CLOUD

Toward what star are you growing,
my son, toward what early morning star?
Tell me, whisper in my ear,
whether there is time still,
for me and that cloud, that high cloud,
to go with you.

NUMA FOTOGRAFIA

Não sejas como a névoa, nem quimera.
Demora-te, demora-te assim:
faz do olhar
tempo sem tempo, espaço
limpo — do deserto ou do mar.

IN A PHOTOGRAPH

Don't be like the mist or a chimera.
Just stay, just stay like this:
make of your gaze
time without time, clean
space — of desert or of sea.

O NOME DA TERRA

Já sobre o meu peito não demoras
os pés miúdos, já a breve
dança dos dedos troca de cabelo,
porque tu cresces, cresces inclinado
para a difícil flor da nossa idade.
És agora o outro nome da terra,
ou simplesmente da eternidade.

A NAME FOR EARTH

Your tiny feet no longer linger
on my chest, the fleeting
dance of fingers has found new hair,
for you are growing, growing bent
toward the difficult flower of our age.
Now you are the other name for earth,
or simply for eternity.

COM AS MAÇÃS

As crianças chegam com as maçãs.
Vêm do sul,
os choupos brancos sabem o seu nome.
Também as gaivotas as conhecem:
aposto que foram elas,
estas ciganas das areias,
quem lhes mostrou o caminho.
Chegam com as maçãs:
as crianças, as abelhas.

WITH APPLES

Children arrive with apples.
They come from the south,
the white poplars know their names.
The sea gulls also know:
I'll bet that's who it was,
those gypsies of the sand,
who showed them the way.
They arrive with apples:
the children, the bees.

CIDADE

O filho pela mão, vamos por estas ruas
esconjurando sombras, convocando
dunas, potros, o sol ainda fresco,
os cachorros latindo de alegria.
Meus olhos vão à frente farejando,
enquanto a mão dele ilumina a minha.

CITY

The child's hand in mine, we go along these streets,
exorcising shadows, summoning forth
dunes, colts, a sun still fresh,
puppies yapping for pure joy.
My eyes go ahead sniffing,
while his hand gives light to mine.

COM OS JUNCOS

Elas crescem, as crianças.
Crescem com os juncos,
com os mastros.
Crescem no meu coração esburacado.
Só as crianças não morrem.
E os gatos.

WITH THE RUSHES

They are growing, the children.
They are growing with the rushes,
with the masts.
They are growing in my threadbare heart.
Only children do not die.
And cats.

MATINALMENTE

Com a luz, com a cal
do verão entornada pela casa,
com essa música
tão amada e bárbara,
com a púrpura correndo
de colina em colina,
fazer uma coroa —
e de lágrimas cheia a taça
sagrar-te príncipe da vida.

EARLY IN THE MORNING

With light, with the white-wash
of summer spilling over the houses,
with this music,
so beloved and barbarous,
with purple flowing
from hill to hill,
to make a crown —
and with a tear-filled goblet
consecrate you prince of life.

Cumplicidades do Verão

Complicities of Summer

A CASA

No meu corpo uma casa se levanta,
sem portas, sem paredes, sem telhado:
entrasse o mar por ela ouviria as sereias,
fosse outra vez verão seria só orvalho.

THE HOUSE

A house is rising up here in my body,
without doors, without walls, without a roof;
should the sea come in, I would hear the sirens,
were it summer once again, there would just be dew.

DO LADO DO VERÃO

Vinha do sul ou dum verso de Homero.
Como dormir, depois de ter ouvido
o mar o mar o mar na sua boca?

FROM SUMMER'S SIDE

He came from the south or from a line of Homer's.
How can I sleep, after having heard
the sea the sea the sea there in his mouth?

PERTO DO MAR

O corpo sabe.
O corpo não esqueceu ainda
a direcção do sol:
fará a casa perto do mar,
fiel ao quase adolescente
coração da água.
As mãos acesas — altas, altas.

CLOSE TO THE SEA

The body knows.
The body has not yet forgotten
the direction of the sun:
it will make its home close to the sea,
faithful to the almost youthful
heart of the water.
Its hands aflame — higher, higher.

CUMPLICIDADE DO VERÃO

Mal nos conhecíamos, mas a infância
é cúmplice do verão:
vinhas do rio, das manhãs
onde nadámos juntos e subimos
aos freixos altos: via-te
balouçar num ramo frágil rindo,
ou saltar atrás das rãs — o corpo nu
cravado nos meus olhos como um espinho.

COMPLICITY OF SUMMER

We scarcely knew each other, but childhood
is accomplice to the summer:
you came from the river, from those mornings
where we swam together and climbed
the tall ash trees: I watched you
swinging from a fragile branch in laughter,
or leaping after frogs — your naked body
nailed in my eyes like a thorn.

RENTE AO CHÃO

Sem nenhuma razão a voz rompia,
a rasteirinha voz tão rente à vida
que se confunde com a luz do chão,
a luz de março rastejando ainda.

CLOSE TO THE GROUND

For no reason at all the voice broke forth,
a little voice creeping on so close to life
it could be taken for the ground's own light,
the light of March still crawling slowly on.

MORADA

A primeira casa não era ainda a casa:
não chega a ser morada.
Na outra, mais pequena, onde ninguém
perguntava que idade tinha
ou se o verão já passara
ou o cão mordia,
a manhã estava à janela.
Essa era a casa, o sol onde ardia.

HOME

The first house still was not the house:
it never quite became a home.
In the other, smaller one, where no one
asked how old I was
or if the summer had already passed
or if the dog would bite,
the morning was there at the window.
That was the house, the sun where I burned.

O SORRISO

Creio que foi o sorriso,
o sorriso foi quem abriu a porta.
Era um sorriso com muita luz
lá dentro, apetecia
entrar nele, tirar a roupa, ficar
nu dentro daquele sorriso.
Correr, navegar, morrer naquele sorriso.

THE SMILE

I think it was the smile,
it was the smile who opened the door.
It was a smile with light, much light
inside, I longed to
enter it, take off my clothes, and stay,
naked there within that smile.
To run, to sail, to die within that smile.

OS PÊSSEGOS

Lembram adolescentes nus:
a doirada pele das nádegas
com marcas de carmim, a penugem
leve, mais encrespada e fulva
em torno do sexo distendido
e fácil, vulnerável aos desejos
de quem só o contempla e não ousa
aproximar dos flancos matinais
a crepuscular lentidão dos dedos.

PEACHES

Like naked youths:
the golden skin of their buttocks,
with traces of carmine, their down
light, crinkled and tawnier
around an extended and easy
sex, vulnerable to the desires
of one who only gazed and didn't dare
approach the early morning flanks
with the twilit slowness of his fingers.

CORPO

O mar — sempre que toco
um corpo é o mar que sinto
onda a onda
contra a palma da mão.
Vésper está agora
tão próxima que já não posso
perder-me naquela infatigável
ondulação.

BODY

The sea — whenever I touch
a body the sea is what I feel
wave after wave
against the palm of my hand.
The evening star is now
so close I cannot any longer
lose myself in that unflagging
undulation.

A PEQUENA VAGA

Mar de pequena vaga e céu azul:
a irrupção das frésias entre a multidão,
orvalhadas ainda de luz insegura,
faz destas ruas um jardim do sul.

SMALL SEAS

Small seas and a blue sky:
an irruption of freesias in the midst of the crowd,
dewy still with the uncertain light,
turns these streets into a garden of the south.

A LUZ DO PÁTIO

Deixas a luz do pátio acesa,
a porta aberta — que esperas ainda?
Amas agora com amor dobrado
a vida, o suor misturado ao sal
da saliva, o rumor
das águas no sol das sementes,
a treva do cabelo incendiada
nas mãos outra vez adolescentes.

THE PATIO LIGHT

You leave the patio light on
and the door ajar — what are you still hoping for?
Now with a doubled love you love
life, sweat mixing with the salt
of saliva, the sound
of waters in the sun of the seeds,
the darkness of hair set aflame
in hands once again made young.

AO LUME

Nem sempre o homem é um lugar triste.
Há noites em que o sorriso
dos anjos
o torna habitável e leve:
com a cabeça no teu regaço
é um cão ao lume a correr às lebres.

BY THE FIRE

Man is not always a place of sorrow.
There are nights in which the smile
of angels
makes him habitable and light:
with his head in your lap
he's a dog by the fire chasing after hares.

OUTRA VEZ

Outra vez as mãos, meu deus, as mãos,
a porosa morada do verão,
o copo de água fresca como folha
de álamo,
o golpe de martelo
quebrando as hastes do silêncio.

AGAIN

Again the hands, my god, the hands,
porous home of summer,
cup of cool water like the leaf
of a poplar,
blow of a hammer
breaking the stalks of silence.

SOBRE A TERRA

Sei que estou vivo e cresço sobre a terra.
Não porque tenha mais poder,
nem mais saber, nem mais haver.
Como lábio que suplica outro lábio,
como pequena e branca chama
de silêncio,
como sopro obscuro do primeiro crepúsculo,
sei que estou vivo, vivo
sobre o teu peito, sobre os teus flancos,
e cresço para ti.

UPON THE EARTH

I know that I'm alive and that I grow upon the earth.
And not because I have more power,
or more knowledge, or more wherewithal.
Like a lip that pleads for another lip,
like the small, white flame
of silence,
like the dark whiff of earliest dawn,
I know that I'm alive, alive
upon your chest, upon your flanks,
and that I grow toward you.

OS GIRASSÓIS

Assim fremente e nua,
a luz só pode ser dos girassóis.
Estou tão orgulhoso
por esta flor difícil ter entrado pela casa.
É talvez o último verão,
tão feito de abandono é meu desejo.
Mas estou orgulhoso dos girassóis.
Como se fora seu irmão.

SUNFLOWERS

Trembling like this and naked,
the light can only be of sunflowers.
I am so proud
this difficult flower has come into my house.
Perhaps this is the last summer,
so slack the weave of my desire.
But I am proud of the sunflowers.
As if I were their brother.

CONTIGO

Sou eu, sou eu que não durmo,
contigo nos sentidos.
Sinto-te caminhar sobre as águas
do meu corpo — não sejas queimadura
nem boca do deserto.
Nenhum amor é estéril, um filho
pode ser uma estrela ou ser um verso.

WITH YOU

It's me, it's me who can't sleep
with you in all my senses.
I feel you walking on the waters
of my body — be neither burn
nor desert mouth.
No love is sterile, a son
can be a star, a line of poetry.

AS AMORAS

O meu país sabe às amoras bravas
no verão.
Ninguém ignora que não é grande,
nem inteligente, nem elegante o meu país,
mas tem esta voz doce
de quem acorda cedo para cantar nas silvas.
Raramente falei do meu país, talvez
nem goste dele, mas quando um amigo
me traz amoras bravas
os seus muros parecem-me brancos,
reparo que também no meu país o céu é azul.

BLACKBERRIES

My country tastes of wild blackberries
in summer.
No one fails to see my country
is neither vast, nor wise, nor elegant,
but it does have that sweet voice
of one who rises early to sing amongst the brambles.
Rarely have I spoken of my country, maybe
I don't even like it, but when a friend
brings me wild blackberries,
its walls seem white to me,
and I realize that here, too, in my own land,
        the sky is blue.

A PUPILA NUA

A luz é sempre a mesma, sempre:
furtiva no flanco das cabras,
crua na coroa dos cardos,
fremente na rasteirinha
relva do teu corpo e nas dunas,
sempre a mesma, a pupila nua.

THE NAKED PUPIL

Light is always the same, always:
furtive on the flanks of goats,
raw on the crown of the thistles,
trembling on the creeping
grasses of your body and on the dunes,
always the same, the pupil naked.

CARDOS

Este é o lugar onde só o lume
não demora a florir,
onde o verão abdica
de ser metáfora para arder
até ao fim.

THISTLES

This is the place where only fire
does not delay in flowering,
where summer abdicates
its being metaphor, to burn
unto the end.

O PEQUENO PERSA

É um pequeno persa
azul o gato deste poema.
Como qualquer outro, o meu
amor por esta alminha é materno:
uma carícia minha lambe-lhe o pêlo,
outra põe-lhe o sol entre as patas
ou uma flor à janela.
Com unhas e dentes e obstinação
transforma em festa a minha vida.
Quer-se dizer, o que me resta dela.

THE LITTLE PERSIAN

A little Blue Persian,
the cat of this poem.
Like any other, my
love for this small soul is motherly:
one of my caresses licks his fur,
another puts the sun between his paws
or a flower in the window.
With nails and teeth and obstinacy
he turns my life into a joy.
That is to say, what's left of it.

A FIGUEIRA

Não tenho mãos para o azul.
Sonho com o mar
que não está longe mas não vejo
arder.
Só a sombra parece estar em casa
debaixo dos meus ramos:
canta baixinho enquanto se descalça.

THE FIG TREE

I don't have hands for the blue.
I dream of the sea
which isn't far, but I don't see
it burn.
Only shadow seems to be at home
beneath my branches:
softly it sings, while taking off its shoes.

EXEMPLOS

Havia ali um cursinho do água,
muros caídos sílaba a sílaba,
um olhar que na fuga se faz ave,
o apagado coração do lume —
são exemplos, só exemplos, da língua.

INSTANCES

There used to be a rivulet over there,
walls fallen syllable by syllable,
a look which fleeing turns into a bird,
the snuffed out heart of the fire —
instances, just instances, of language.

RESSACA

A violência fresca do vinho;
os sulcos da ressaca; o silvo matinal
do pastor, mais propício à arte
que toda a música das esferas;
este orgulho de ter no coração
o leite entornado das estrelas.

RECEDING SURF

The cool violence of wine;
the furrows of receding surf; the morning whistle
of the shepherd, more propitious for art
than all the music of the spheres;
this pride at having in one's heart
the spilled milk of the stars.

O FALCÃO

Despeço-me do verão junto às águas
frias do norte — sobre os rios
já outros
disseram o que havia a dizer;
os de Sião não são os meus,
os de Babilónia também não;
eu sou o falcão mais jovem,
sou doutros ares, doutro céu,
deixai-me arder.

THE FALCON

I take leave of summer beside the cold
waters of the north — about rivers
others have already
said what there was to say;
those of Zion are not mine,
nor those of Babylon;
I am the youngest falcon,
I am of other mountains, other skies,
let me blaze.

LUGARES DO OUTONO

Outono, labirinto de silvas,
de sílabas, digo, pupila lenta,
rio de inumeráveis águas
e de amieiros altos onde canta
a derradeira luz das cigarras,
de vidro ainda, e leve, e branca.

AUTUMN PLACES

Autumn, labyrinth of sibilance,
of syllables, I mean, slow pupil,
river of unmeasured waters
and of tall alders where
the last light of the cicadas sings,
still glassy, feathery, and white.

MESMO EM RUÍNA

É tão antiga a chuva na vidraça.
Vem do pequeno bosque onde o verão
mordia os flancos da água.
O que no coração tarda
a morrer é a luz mesmo em ruína.
A sumptuosa seda do outono.
A doçura, o sal da língua.

EVEN IN RUINS

So very old, that rain upon the window.
It comes from the small wood where summer
was nipping at the water's flanks.
What puts off dying in the heart
is light even in ruins.
The sumptuous silk of autumn.
The sweetness, the salt of the tongue.

CASA VELHA

Não é a primeira vez que me queixo,
ninguém me escuta.
Esta noite a chuva entrou-me pelos ossos
e não há quem acenda o lume.
Quem partiu levou consigo
o rapazito com olhos de coral,
deixando atrás de si a porta aberta.

THE OLD HOUSE

It’s not the first time that I complain,
no one listens to me.
Tonight the rain got to my very bones
and there is no one to light the fire.
The one who left took along
the little boy with eyes of coral,
leaving the door open behind him.

OUTONO

O outono vem vindo, chegam melancolias,
cavam fundo no corpo,
instalam-se nas fendas; às vezes
por aí ficam com a chuva
apodrecendo;
ou então deixam marcas, as putas,
difíceis de apagar, de tão negras,
duras.

AUTUMN

Autumn is drawing near, sorrows arrive,
dig deep into the body,
install themselves in the cracks; sometimes
they stay out there with the rain,
rotting;
or, then again, they leave their mark, the bitches,
tough to erase, so black,
so hard.

DESPEDIDA

Junho chegara ao fim, a magoada
luz dos jacarandás, que me pousava
nos ombros, era agora o que tinha
para repartir contigo,
e um coração desmantelado
que só aos gatos servirá de abrigo.

LEAVE-TAKING

June had come to its end, and the bruised
light of the jacarandas, settling
on my shoulders, was what I now had
to share with you,
that and a dismantled heart
which soon would serve to harbor only cats.

SEM TI

É um fardo aos ombros
o corpo, sem ti.
Até o amarelo
dos girassóis se tornou cruel.
Não invento nada,
na arte de olhar
a luz é cúmplice da pele.

WITHOUT YOU

It's a load on my shoulders,
this body, without you.
Even the yellow
of sunflowers has turned cruel.
I invent nothing;
in the art of looking,
light is the accomplice of the flesh.

O DESEJO

O desejo, o aéreo e luminoso
e magoado desejo latia ainda;
não sei bem em que lugar
do corpo em declínio mas latia;
bastava abrir os olhos para ouvir
o nasalado ardor da sua voz:
era a manhã trepando às dunas,
era o céu de cal onde o sul começa,
era por fim o mar à porta — o mar,
o mar, pois só o mar cantava assim.

DESIRE

Desire, airy and luminous
and bruised desire, throbbing still;
I don't know exactly in what part
of this sinking body, but it was throbbing;
just opening my eyes was enough for me to hear
the nasal ardor of its voice:
it was morning mounting the dunes,
it was the white-washed sky where the south begins,
it was, finally, the sea at my doorstep — the sea,
the sea, for only the sea could sing like that.

O QUE NÃO PODE MORRER

Diz, diz uma vez mais o que não pode
morrer:
a luz, que no sul é inocente
e trepa aos pinheiros;
o trote miúdo das manhãs de junho;
a azul a pique do falcão;
as dunas, com sinais ainda
doutro verão para levar à boca.

WHAT CANNOT DIE

Say, say once again what cannot
die;
light, which in the south is innocent
and climbs the trunks of pines;
the tiny trot of mornings in June;
the blue swoop of the hawk;
the dunes, with traces still
of another summer to lift to my mouth.

QUANDO JUNHO VOLTAR

A quem deste a mão, confiaste
a sua seda? O ardor
do verão caiu ao rio,
a tão amada voz perdeu
o seu rebanho.
Quando junho voltar,
quem sabe onde fará a casa?

WHEN JUNE RETURNS

To whom did you give your hand, confide
its silk? The heat
of summer fell to the river,
the much loved voice lost
its flock.
When June returns,
who knows where it will build its house?

AINDO ESPERO

Seja como for, ainda espero
dos altos muros ver a dança
das nuvens sobre o rio,
as gloriosas flores desfraldar
a louca cabeleira.
Eram a casa do verão, os girassóis.
A derradeira.

STILL I HOPE

No matter what, still I hope
to see from high on the walls the dance
of the clouds upon the river,
the glorious flowers shaking loose
their insane tresses.
They were the house of summer, those sunflowers.
The final one.

CASUALMENTE

Vinha do mar, a sua boca ardia;
só casualmente passou por aqui;
como o tordo branco, ou a cotovia.

BY CHANCE

He came from the sea, his mouth burning;
it was just by chance that he passed this way;
like the song-thrush, or the lark.

Rosa do Mundo

Rose of the World

A PAIXÃO

Levanto a custo os olhos da página;
ardem;
ardem cegos de tanta neve.
Faz dó esta paixão pelo silêncio,
pelo sussurro do silêncio,
pelo ardor
do silêncio que só os dedos adivinham.
Cegos, também.

PASSION

With an effort, I lift my eyes from the page;
they burn;
burn, blind from so much snow.
It gives pain, this passion for silence,
for the whisper of silence,
for the heat
of silence that only fingers can divine.
Blind, as well.

SUL

Era verão, havia o muro.
Na praça, a única evidência
eram os pombos, o ardor
da cal. De repente
o silêncio sacudiu as crinas,
correu para o mar.
Pensei: devíamos morrer assim.
Assim: explodir no ar.

SOUTH

It was summer, there was a wall.
In the square, the only thing in evidence
were pigeons, the heat
of white-washed walls. Suddenly
silence shook its mane
and ran to the sea.
I thought: that's how we ought to die.
Just like that: exploding in the air.

TODA A MÚSICA

Sem ser inverno ainda
o cheiro tímido é já da chuva.
Sentia o mar subir, tinha as mãos
prontas para o levar à boca:
toda a música
era só aquela rebentação.

ALL MUSIC

Without it being winter yet
the timid scent already is of rain.
I felt the sea rise, my hands
ready to lift it to my mouth:
all music —
just that breaking surf.

EPITÁFIO

Janeiro não é mês para morrer,
nem o mar nem a luz são
propícios — parece que vai nevar.
Mesmo assim, tu decidiste
que seria a última, esta tarde:
vias uma criança escalar o muro
do verão, e sorrias — há muito tempo.

EPITAPH

January is not a month for dying,
neither the sea nor the light are
conducive — it looks like snow.
Even so, you decided
that this would be the last, this afternoon:
you saw a child scale the wall
of summer, and you smiled — long ago.

A VISITA

Atravessou a rua, empurrou a porta,
os seus passos crepitam no luz frouxa:
era como na infância a morte,
assim alta, assim branca, assim rouca.

THE VISIT

He crossed the street, pushed in the door,
his footsteps crackled in the weak light:
it was like death in childhood,
just as tall, as white, as hoarse.

SEM MEMÓRIA

Haverá para os dias sem memória
outro nome que não seja morte?
Morte das coisas limpas, leves:
manhã rente às colinas,
a luz do corpo levada aos lábios,
os primeiros lilases do jardim.
Haverá outro nome para o lugar
onde não há lembrança de ti?

UNREMEMBERED

Will there be for unremembered days
another name than death?
Death of limpid things, things light:
morning hugging the hills,
the light of the body lifted to the lips,
the first lilacs of the garden.
Will there be another name for the place
where there will be no memory of you?

ROSA DO MUNDO

Rosa. Rosa do mundo.
Queimada.
Suja de tanta palavra.

Primeiro orvalho sobre o rosto.
Que foi pétala
a pétala lenço do soluços.

Obscena rosa. Repartida.
Amada.
Boca ferida, sopro de ninguém.

Quase nada.

ROSE OF THE WORLD

Rose. Rose of the world.
Burnt.
Filthy from so many words.

First dew upon my face.
Petal by petal, it was
a handkerchief of sobs.

Obscene rose. Shared.
Loved.
Wounded mouth, nobody's breath.

Almost nothing.

About the Translator

Alexis Levitin is the winner of an NEA Translation Award, a Gulbenkian Foundation Award, a New York State Council on the Arts Translation Award, the Fernando Pessoa Translation Award from Columbia University, a Wheatland Foundation grant, and a Betty A. Coladay Award for his translations of the works of Eugénio de Andrade. These de Andrade translations have appeared in well over 100 literary magazines and have resulted in seven books to date.

A Professor of English at SUNY-Plattsburgh in upstate New York, he has also taught at Dartmouth, Tufts, Colby, Denison, and at universities in Brazil and Portugal.

"Alexis Levitin, the premier translator of Portuguese poetry into English and of several volumes of Eugénio de Andrade, Portugal's leading live poet, has now made available de Andrade's recent volume, the magical sequence, *Solar Matter*, a passionate exchange between the sun and its chief focus, the body, or its product, desire."

Professor Theodore Weiss, Princeton University
Editor and publisher, *Quarterly Review of Literature*

"It is sheer delight to come across the poems of Eugénio de Andrade again in Alexis Levitin's sensitive and lyrical translations. De Andrade reduces all our most profound disturbances to the simplest, truest, and wisest images, in which man and nature become irrevocably one. These are poems about aging and dying and above all about the intensity of love itself, a burden and a joy, which does not diminish with age in the least but grows ever more profound."

C.W. Truesdale, author of *Doctor Vertigo*
Editor and publisher, *New Rivers Press*

Titles Available from QED Press

Poetry

Matéria Solar / Solar Matter *by Eugénio de Andrade*
Translated by Alexis Levitin

Stunning poems by one of Europe's most famous writers in "Alexis Levitin's sensitive and lyrical translation."

$12.95 128 pages (paper) $5^1/_2$" x 7" 0-936609-34-6

A Mendocino Portfolio *by Cynthia Frank & Hannes Krebs*

Stark poetry and evocative black and white photography.

$17.95 88 pages (case) 10" x 8" 0-936609-12-5

Messages: New and Selected Poems *by Luke Breit*
Poetry highly praised by Ernesto Cardenal and Norman Mailer.

$8.95 136 pages (paper) $5^1/_2$" x $8^1/_2$" 0-936609-17-6

Art

Paris Connections: African American Artists in Paris

For this book, editors Asake Bomani and Belvie Rooks won a *Before Columbus Foundation American Book Award.* Bilingual (French/English), full-color reproductions, biographies, bibliography, index.

$30.00 128 pages (paper) $8^1/_2$" x 10" 0-936609-25-7

Paris Connections: African and Caribbean Artists in Paris

Editors Asake Bomani and Belvie Rooks present another collection of bilingual (French/English) essays on African and Caribbean artists in Paris. Full-color reproductions, biographies, index.

$14.95 64 pages (paper) $8^1/_2$" x $8^1/_2$" 0-936609-26-5

Creative Nonfiction

Iron House *by Jerome Washington*

Winner of the 1994 *Western States Arts Federation Book Award for Creative Nonfiction,* this much-praised book about the "con artists, sex addicts, psychotics and dreamers" who inhabit our prisons is both funny and searing.

$18.95 176 pages (case) $5^1/_2$" x $8^1/_2$" 0-936609-33-8

Fiction

Tales From The Mountain *by Miguel Torga*

Ivana Carlsen translates this extraordinary collection of powerful short stories by Portugal's Nobel Prize nominee.

$12.99	160 pages (paper)	5½“ x 8½”	0-936609-23-0
$21.99	160 pages (case)	5½“ x 8½”	0-936609-24-9

The Man Who Owned the Hogs *by Leonard Dugger*

A savage, elegant, iconoclastic satire that attacks the foundations of religion while telling a gripping, ultimately tragic story.

$21.95	208 pages (case)	5½“ x 8½”	1-879384-18-3

Psychology/Counseling/Health

Finding the Way Home: A Compassionate Approach to Illness
by Gayle Heiss

Anyone touched by health concerns will treasure *Finding the Way Home*. The inner world of illness is portrayed with clarity and compassion. A guide to living wisely, no matter one's state of health.

$24.95	320 pages (case)	6" x 9"	0-936609-35-4

Defending Against the Enemy: Coping with Parkinson's Disease
by Eric Morgan

Scientist Eric Morgan and his wife both suffered from the "enemy," Parkinson's Disease. A journal of the years "at war" coupled with scientific research, medical experimentation and practical advice.

$12.95	128 pages (paper)	5½“ x 8½”	0-936609-36-2

Listening with Different Ears: Counseling People Over 60
by James Warnick

A practical guide for therapists, social workers, ministers and family members who want to help seniors in emotional distress.

$19.50	224 pages (paper)	6" x 9"	0-936609-28-1
$24.95	224 pages (case)	6" x 9"	0-936609-31-1

The Collected Works of Lydia Sicher: An Adlerian Perspective

Adele K. Davidson edits this definitive work of one whose "contribution to Individual Psychology is enormous and brilliant."
— Dr. Harold Mosak, Adler School of Professional Psychology

$24.95	572 pages (paper)	6" x 9"	0-936609-22-2

Biography

Closing the Circle: An American Family in China, *by Elsie Landstrom*

More than sixty years ago, Elsie Landstrom sailed from New England to China where she met Hyla Doc, the woman who brought Western medicine to victims of warfare, disease, and malnutrition.

$16.95 176 pages (paper) 6" x 9" 0-936609-19-2

Hyla Doc: Surgeon in China through War and Revolution, 1924-1949, *edited by Elsie Landstrom*

The memoirs of the surgeon who treated the victims of the Rape of Nanking in war-torn China.

$12.95 310 pages (paper) 6" x 9" 0-936609-19-2

Hyla Doc in Africa, 1950-1961, *edited by Elsie Landstrom*

Hyla Doc brings her unique blend of medical skill and compassion to the bush country of Liberia.

$10.50 104 pages (paper) 6" x 9" 0-936609-32-X

Business

Take This Job and Sell It! The Recruiter's Handbook
by Richard Mackie

Richard Mackie, guru to headhunters, describes, step-by-step, how to earn $100,000 a year at home by recruiting and placing professionals at mid-sized companies.

$24.95 176 pages (paper) 8½" x 11" 0-936609-30-3

Available at your local bookstore or from

QED Press
155 Cypress Street, Fort Bragg, CA 95437
(800) 773-7782 or (707) 964-9520
Fax (707) 964-7531
e-mail: qedpress@mcn.org
website: cypresshouse.com